# *The Electric Bike Manifesto*

# The Electric Bike Manifesto

How Electric Bicycles Can Save Our World
(If We Let Them)

Micah Toll

Copyright © 2021 Micah Toll

Cover design by Etai Berman

All rights reserved.

No part of this book may be reproduced in any form or by any electronic or mechanical means including information storage and retrieval systems, without permission in writing from the author. The only exception is by a reviewer, who may quote short excerpts in a review.

ISBN-13: 978-0-9899067-3-9

*To my wife Sapir, who has somehow yet to tire of me*

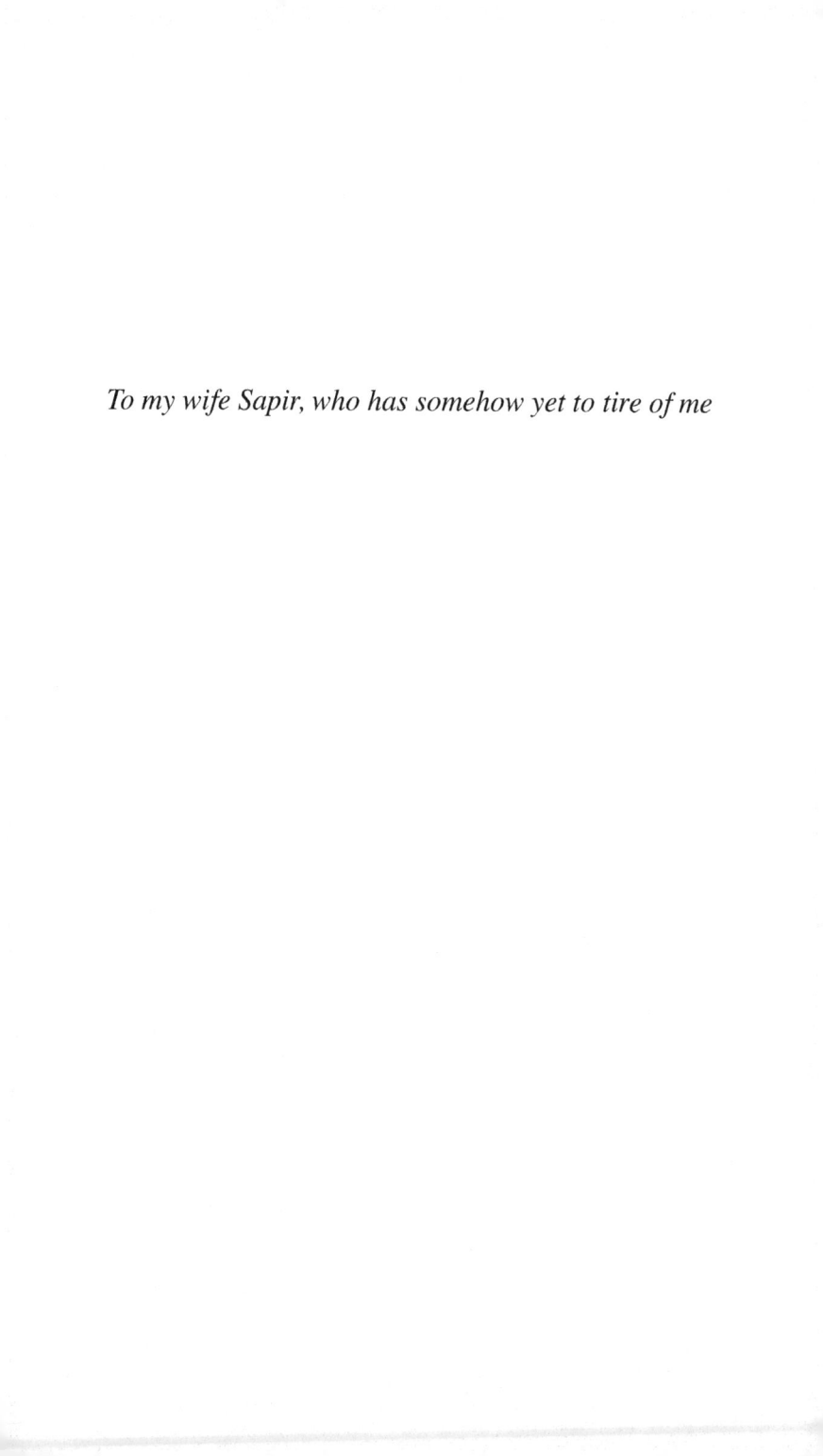

# Table of Contents

Chapter 1: Facing the problem ..................................................9

Chapter 2: Transportation in our society and its future......15

Chapter 3: Save your life, not just the planet .....................27

Chapter 4: Embracing a massive shift towards e-bikes ......37

Chapter 5: What can you do about it? ...................................47

Chapter 6: Finding the right e-bike.........................................53

    Electric city bikes...............................................................55

    Folding electric bikes.........................................................56

    Electric mountain bikes.....................................................57

    Fat tire electric bikes .........................................................57

    Electric cruiser bikes..........................................................58

    Cargo/utility e-bikes..........................................................59

    Electric road bikes..............................................................59

    Electric mopeds ..................................................................60

Chapter 7: Are e-bikes the only answer?...............................63

Chapter 8: Common arguments against e-bikes..................71

Chapter 9: Where do we go from here?.................................85

# Chapter 1: Facing the problem

Our world is in bad shape.

It is being destroyed right before our eyes.

Yes, we have learned to live with it. Anyone staring at a problem long enough without seeing change will eventually learn to adapt. And so many of us have reached a tenuous equilibrium - a point where our reality more or less works for us on a day to day basis and we accept that this is the way it is. But the world is rife with problems, no matter how hard we ignore them.

Our cities have become crowded, dirty and gridlocked urban jungles in which millions of people waste billions of hours simply trying to move around each other in pursuit of their lives. Our transportation systems are based on inefficient and outdated technologies and strategies that better serve a few wealthy industries than the actual individuals relying on such transportation.

Our planet has been pillaged for its resources to enable this unproductive, wasteful system. Corporations have convinced us that we all need large, polluting vehicles in order to go about our days. Then they've destroyed the earth by extracting its non-renewable resources, all the while convincing us to pay them for these resources that are required by design to make our vehicles work. And then we have to choke down the toxic fumes that they created - or that we were forced to create - when we use the products that they convinced us we needed.

Our fellow humans have grown fatter, sicker and to a large degree lazier as a result. Many of us already spend most of our working days immobilized at a desk. Theoretically, the act of going to and leaving work would be two of the few active moments in our daily routine, welcomed as a way to break up the lethargy we experience all day. But the design of our transportation system means that nearly all of us are nonsensically just as immobile while we move around as we are after arriving at work. We move from our beds to our cars to our desks, then back to our cars, then to our couches and finally to our beds. Our sedentary habits have combined with an increasing overabundance of easily available junk food to create an unhealthy lifestyle that has led to skyrocketing rates of obesity, heart disease, diabetes and death.

If that wasn't bad enough, our personal time isn't even safe from the current grim state of the world. The last few generations have seen wholesale erosion of personal, leisure and family time. Nine to five jobs are a relic of the past as personal and leisure time give way to the modern responsibilities of life, inside and outside of work. Cultural shifts around the world have seen personal and family time sacrificed in the pursuit of (or sometimes the charade of) improved productivity.

But perhaps the biggest tragedy of all isn't the current state of our world, it's that we've largely accepted this as our fate. With the exception of a small group of well-meaning individuals and organizations, the world's public has accepted the destruction of our planet, an upside-down transportation system, and the steady decline of our collective physical and mental health as the status quo.

But despair not, dear reader. For even though the picture of our world that I've painted appears dark, there lies a single silver bullet that can save us all from this dystopia in which we've slowly marched ourselves into. I am speaking, of course, of the humble electric bicycle.

The electric bicycle, for those not yet fortunate enough to have met this wonderful contraption, is nothing more than a typical pedal bicycle, but with the addition of an electric motor and battery to assist the rider. Many function identically to a typical pedal bicycle, differing only in reducing the effort needed to travel the same distance. Riders of electric bicycles can travel faster and farther without getting as tired.

Many variations of electric bicycles, or e-bikes, exist today. Different laws from country to country have resulted in some electric bicycles that are barely more powerful than the legs of an average rider to e-bikes that can provide the equivalent assistance of several professional cyclists pedaling simultaneously for you.

Some electric bicycles only engage the motor when the rider pedals. These are often known as pedal assist e-bikes or pedelecs. Other electric bicycles are fitted with hand-activated throttles similar to a motorcycle or moped. This hand throttle allows the e-bike to be operated without requiring the rider to actually engage the pedals.

Just like standard pedal bicycles, e-bikes are available in several styles for different types of riding, such as urban or metro e-bikes, off-road e-bikes, folding e-bikes, cargo e-bikes and many more specialized variants.

Despite the many different styles and variations of electric bicycles on the market, they all share one important unifying factor: an effective alternative form of transportation that can play a large role in solving many of our world's most urgent plights.

Electric bicycles are one of the most efficient forms of transportation in existence. For commuters that currently travel by private car, e-bikes offer an equally effective transportation alternative that expends a tiny fraction of the energy required by either gas-powered or electric cars. But while the main argument for the use of e-bikes is often centered on their energy efficiency and lack of polluting emissions, these electric two-wheelers offer a myriad of additional benefits.

In crowded cities, e-bikes can often reduce commute times compared to larger vehicles. They reduce traffic and congestion on roads, benefiting all drivers. They provide additional movement and exercise, which are both critical to maintaining proper mental and physical health. E-bike riding also makes for a wonderful recreational activity, and can even help inject some much-needed fun into purely utilitarian transportation such as daily commuting and errand running.

All of these benefits are nice by themselves, but they also combine to offer solutions to many of the most pressing problems facing society today. Don't believe me? In the next few chapters, we'll explore these and many more benefits of electric bicycles. We'll dive deeper into the way these tools can be used to solve some of our world's largest problems today, and we'll explore the practical considerations that will be necessary to actually achieve these solutions in a relatively short time frame.

# Chapter 2: Transportation in our society and its future

I've never liked the term "climate change" because it simply isn't a good enough description. It doesn't reflect the gravity of the situation. Our world is staring down the barrel of a climate catastrophe. And that's not hyperbole. A disaster isn't just one of many possible scenarios. It is the current outcome we are actively heading toward.

Our best chances at staving off climate-related disasters such as rising seas, massive plant and animal die-offs and scarcity of drinking water in many areas lie in the reduction of carbon emissions. According to the United States Environmental Protection Agency, transportation represents the single largest share of carbon emissions in the US, followed closely by electricity generation.[1] Transportation also accounts for the second-largest share of carbon emissions in Europe, surpassed only by energy production, according to the European Environmental Agency.[2]

Shifting transportation towards alternative methods that produce lower carbon emissions will have one of the largest impacts towards slowing and (if we are lucky) eventually reversing current climate change trends. Many of the efforts in this area are currently focused on shifting towards the electrification of transportation. This is mostly centered around personal cars, but other transportation industries such as trucking, shipping, aviation and public transit are also undergoing electrification efforts of varying intensities.

With electricity production currently responsible for nearly as much carbon emissions as transportation, simply shifting the fuel source from fossil fuels to electricity limits the effectiveness of this solution. It is not enough to simply replace gas-powered engines with electric motors.

---

[1] "Inventory of U.S. Greenhouse Gas Emissions and Sinks." *EPA*, Environmental Protection Agency, 11 Feb. 2021, www.epa.gov/ghgemissions/inventory-us-greenhouse-gas-emissions-and-sinks.

[2] "Greenhouse Gas Emissions by Aggregated Sector." *European Environment Agency*, 19 Dec. 2019, www.eea.europa.eu/data-and-maps/daviz/ghg-emissions-by-aggregated-sector-5#tab-dashboard-02.

Now my point here should not be mistaken. Electrification of all applicable transportation is the correct course of action. It is true that electric vehicles are more energy-efficient than gas-powered vehicles. It is also true that electric vehicles produce fewer carbon emissions even when their electricity is produced from power plants that burn fossil fuels. And it is furthermore true that electricity generation is likely to see its share of carbon emissions reduced as more renewable forms such as solar, wind and geothermal increase their share of the sector. But while electrification of all transportation is a critical step in the right direction, it is but the first step in a longer march. Equally important is an absolute *reduction* in the amount of energy used for transportation.

To put it another way, it is not enough for us to make transportation cleaner; it must also be more efficient. That means we must shift towards alternative forms of transportation that use less total energy for the same trip.

Electric bicycles are key to both major strategies related to carbon emission reductions: they shift transportation to cleaner, lower-emission electric drive, and they also reduce the total amount of energy required for that transportation. Electric cars may be highly efficient compared to gas-powered cars, but no amount of electrification can overcome the fact that cars carry thousands of pounds of extra weight around, torpedoing their efficiency compared to lightweight electric bicycles. Critically, electric bicycles provide the bare minimum necessary for an effective form of transportation: a source of locomotion and a structure to support that source. Thus, an electric bicycle rider will likely outweigh his or her vehicle by several times, whereas inversely an electric car may outweigh its driver by several dozens of times.

This is the root of an e-bike's energy efficiency advantage: the vast majority of the energy expended by the e-bike goes into moving the occupant. Any vehicle that outweighs its occupant finds itself in exactly the opposite scenario – most of its energy is contributed to moving the vehicle itself, not the occupant. And no one needs reminding that the entire name of this game is moving the occupant.

The e-bike's energy advantage can be seen clearly in the size of its battery. A typical e-bike battery is roughly the size of a 1-liter bottle of water and grants an e-bike around 40-60 km (25-37 mi) of range. Electric car batteries on the other hand are closer in volume to a refrigerator while providing around 10x the range of an e-bike. It takes no stretch of the imagination to consider that a refrigerator can fit more than 10 bottles of water. And thus even though electric cars may be better at traveling longer ranges, their efficiencies when doing so are horribly wasteful when compared to an electric bicycle.

To use more precise numbers, e-bikes can often be operated with efficiencies ranging from 2-20 Wh per kilometer (the range is quite wide due to the effect of various intensities of pedaling). Electric cars often fall in the range of 150-300 Wh per kilometer. Thus e-bikes can offer consumption rates of between 0.7% to 13% of those from electric cars. In other words, electric bicycles can be anywhere from 8 to 140x more efficient than electric cars. And don't get me started on gas-powered cars.

While it would be unreasonable to expect all car trips to be replaced by e-bike trips, the math is clear: Every car trip that *can* be replaced should be.

E-bikes are simply one of the most energy-efficient forms of transportation that exist, ranking ahead of motorcycles, cars, buses, trains, planes and boats. The only forms of transportation that use less energy than e-bikes are purely human-powered, such as walking, skateboards, kickscooters and pedal bicycles (a subject we will touch on briefly in a later chapter).

Energy efficiency isn't the only argument for e-bike use in urban areas. We're only getting started here. E-bikes hold many advantages in cities that are completely unrelated to their high efficiency.

While the effects of climate change are often too abstract or distant to burden the thoughts of city dwellers on a daily basis, urban grime is a constant reminder of how dirty our transportation system truly is. Simply swipe a finger along a curb or park bench and you're likely to see the effects of vehicle emissions right in front of your eyes. Urban grime consists of pollutants, soot and organic compounds that create a film on outdoor surfaces. The sources for urban grime are numerous, but transportation emissions are considered to play a leading role.

I went to college in Pittsburgh during a period when the city was undergoing a massive effort to literally wash away years of industrial emissions. Famous buildings such as the 163-meter (535-foot) tall Cathedral of Learning were scrubbed clean in a painstaking process, removing decades of black soot and revealing the beautiful stone architecture underneath. It had been decades since anyone had seen just how beautiful the city could be – it had simply been covered in grime.

Urban grime isn't just an eyesore, it is a health hazard as well. A 2020 study performed by the Department of Chemistry at Syracuse University found that urban grime is likely responsible for making cities hotter by absorbing sunlight and that it may participate in photochemical reactions that impact both air and water quality.[3]

Electric cars are a great step in the right direction for reducing urban grime, but their high purchase prices have limited their adoption. More affordable gas-powered vehicles are still much more prevalent and continue to contribute to high levels of urban grime

---

[3] Kroptavich, Corey R., et al. "Physical and Chemical Characterization of Urban Grime Sampled from Two Cities." *ACS Earth and Space Chemistry*, vol. 4, no. 10, 2020, pp. 1813–1822., doi:10.1021/acsearthspacechem.0c00192.

around the world. Electric bicycles are a much more affordable alternative that can help commuters reduce their energy consumption and their emissions, further curtailing the increase in urban grime.

This leads to another advantage of electric bicycles, the democratization of personal transportation. In many cities, cars are a luxury of the middle and upper class. Private car ownership is simply out of the question for many commuters. It isn't just the high purchase cost of personal cars, though that serves as the first barrier to entry for many low-income families. Other costs such as insurance, gas and even parking – which can be astronomically expensive in many cities – can prevent people from owning vehicles.

This can have additional negative consequences on these already vulnerable groups. Public transportation generally requires commuters to conform to a rigid schedule, complicating other aspects of life such as meals and child care. Public transportation is often of limited usefulness for last-mile journeys, meaning riders often must invest even more time walking to and from transit hubs. As the COVID-19 pandemic demonstrated, public transportation also forces the poorest among us into cramped spaces that put them at higher risk for the spread of diseases.

Once again, electric bicycles provide an attractive solution. Prices vary, but e-bikes are almost universally more affordable than personal cars. Many e-bikes can be purchased for well under $1,000. Financing options also exist that can make e-bikes as affordable as a monthly public transportation pass. By providing this form of transportation freedom, e-bikes can help lower-income commuters travel on their own schedule, follow their own routes and maintain their own personal space.

This is an excellent time to point out yet another uncomfortable transportation fact: personal vehicles are expensive purchases that we have been trained to consider vital, but which are actually often unnecessary. When an individual spends half of a year's salary on a several thousand-pound machine that requires further payment for gas, parking, maintenance and insurance, it's not because the vehicle best serves the consumer. It is because it serves someone else best. As you can probably deduce, the largest benefactors are the executives at the top of their respective industries. Car companies have convinced us that we need to spend vast sums on expensive boxes to carry us to the grocery store for a loaf of bread. While there are certainly trips that require personal cars, many of our daily trips simply do not. They could just as easily be performed in a much more economical and efficient form of transportation. An e-bike can carry you to the local coffee shop or corner store just as easily as a car. In many cases, it can even do so more quickly.

That's actually the final advantage of e-bikes in cities: they aren't just more energy and cost-efficient, they are also more *time-efficient*. In many cities, it is not at all uncommon for an electric bicycle rider to arrive well in advance of car drivers or public transit passengers. The simple reason is that e-bikes are able to more efficiently navigate cities via bike lanes, sidewalks and other shortcuts not available to larger vehicles.

Even as bike lanes become more crowded due to increased cycling rates, e-bikes simply take up less space, allowing more riders to navigate in the same space. A lane of cars one mile (1.6 km) long is likely to include around 200-250 drivers. A lane of e-bikes of equal length could easily contain 1,000 to 1,500 riders. Of course, cars can conceivably carry more than one passenger, which is precisely the goal behind carpooling. But any glance at a rush hour traffic jam will demonstrate how few cars in practice actually carry more than one occupant.

E-bikes take advantage of their small size to quickly navigate crowded cities. When time is money (or even more importantly happiness), arriving at work or home in half of the time can be a huge advantage. Who wouldn't rather spend less time waiting in traffic and more time doing what matters?

Interestingly, reduced commute times are a benefit that everyone can take advantage of, not just e-bike riders. A 2011 study by Belgian consulting company Transport and Mobility Leuven found that when 10% of personal cars in Brussels were replaced by motorcycles, total time losses from road congestion were reduced by

40%.[4] When 25% of cars were replaced by motorcycles, road congestion was eliminated and traffic simply flowed.

These benefits were gained due to a combination of more efficient packing from the smaller vehicle size of motorcycles as well as the ability for motorcycles to filter through traffic, removing them from the line of traffic and effectively taking them out of the equation. When e-bikes replace cars, the effects could be even more pronounced due to even more efficient packing of vehicles as well as e-bikes being completely removed from the road in many areas where they instead ride in specially designated bicycle lanes.

This reduction in congestion offered by a switch to e-bikes not only saves everyone time in their commutes, but it also decreases the total amount of pollution generated by cars waiting in the reduced traffic. Fewer cars idling is better for everyone. And reaping these benefits doesn't even require that many drivers switch to e-bikes. The results of the Brussels study are clear: even a small number of car drivers that switch to two-wheeled vehicles can have massive benefits for all road users with regards to lower congestion and reduced pollution. It is truly one of these magical moments where everyone wins.

---

[4] Ypperman, I. "Commuting by Motorcycle: Impact Analysis." *Transport & Mobility Leuven*, vol. 10.69, 21 Sept. 2011.

It is easy to see that the environmental and economic advantages offered by electric bicycles are vast. Every car that is replaced by an electric bicycle carries with it a measurable environmental, ecological and economical impact. Yet despite these advantages of electric bicycles, of course not every commuter is able to replace a car in their lives with an e-bike. A lucky few may find themselves with the perfect living situation to allow commuting entirely by e-bike, but that likely isn't the majority. We can't simply delete cars from garages and roads, expecting everyone to get by with an e-bike.

Instead, it is important to focus on replacing car *trips* with e-bike trips, as opposed to only ridding commuters of their cars. It would be great to reduce the total number of cars, but the current design of our cities and our societies continues to require the car form factor for longer distance travels and for carrying larger amounts of cargo (though new solutions like car-sharing can help reduce car ownership – another step in the right direction).

By focusing instead on replacing car trips, we can still obtain many of the societal benefits mentioned in the previous pages. Any trip that doesn't require a heavy-wheeled box shouldn't use one. Every local trip that is purely for personal transport should be optimized with the smallest, most energy-efficient vehicle possible. While a twice-monthly grocery store run might need to fill an entire car with food and supplies, the daily ride to work or a coffee shop could be performed on an e-bike.

Choosing the right vehicle for the job can help us reduce the overuse of cars and cut down on their negative impacts.

But if we think a bit more creatively, we may find that even more trips are possible with e-bikes than we originally expected. Even when trips seemingly exceed the ability of an e-bike, perhaps the commuter simply needs to readjust what he or she considers an e-bike to be. Remember that twice-monthly grocery shopping trip that we assumed required a car? That same grocery run can likely be accomplished on a cargo e-bike designed to carry a trunk's worth of shopping bags. A cargo e-bike (or e-trike) can also carry several kids to school or daycare, allowing a parent to leave the minivan or SUV at home.

In this way, even commuters who can't replace a first car with an e-bike can conceivably replace a second car. A two-car family can potentially become a one-car and one-electric bike family. This is of course dependent upon each family and its own specific needs. But as we have seen, many of the benefits of e-bikes affect the entire population even when only adopted by a small portion of the population.

E-bikes are not a complete solution for everybody on their own. But when applied to a large population, they can have huge impacts on a city. As long as a healthy portion of a city's car trips are replaced by e-bike trips, the environmental and economic advantages outlined in this chapter can be immense.

# Chapter 3: Save your life, not just the planet

In the previous chapter, we discussed the practical advantages of electric bicycles as tools of transportation. It can be plainly seen that such advantages, including reduced levels of pollution, lower transportation costs and reduced traffic, are some of the most influential reasons for a mass shift towards electric bicycle-based transportation.

But in addition to the practical benefits of e-bikes as transportation tools, the health benefits of electric bicycle use can not be overstated. These health benefits can have a massive impact on the quality of the lives of individuals as well as an impact on society as a whole.

It may seem counterintuitive, but electric bicycles are actually an excellent form of exercise. There is a misconception that electric bicycles don't require exertion and many old-school cyclists have dismissed e-bikes as a form of "cheating". This misconception has often led to the derision of e-bike riders from both sides. Traditional pedal cyclists will often dismiss e-bike riders as infringing upon their space, unwilling to accept them into their sport or into their bike lanes. On the other hand, drivers often see e-bikes as they would any other bicycle, a slow-moving obstruction on the side of their road.

The truth, as it often does, lies somewhere in the middle. Electric bicycles are legitimate motor vehicles, at least in so far as a bicycle is a type of vehicle and an e-bike includes a motor (legally speaking, most areas do not consider e-bikes to be "motor vehicles" for classification purposes). But e-bikes also provide an excellent opportunity for exercise, and in some cases result in riders getting more exercise than they would on pedal bikes as the e-bike can often allow a rider to stay out riding for longer.

The crux of the matter lies in the pedal-assist nature of an electric bicycle. Temporarily setting aside the issue of throttle-enabled electric bicycles, e-bikes that feature pedal assist are operated by pedaling just as one would on an ordinary bicycle. The e-bike detects the pedal input of the rider through a variety of sensors and in turn activates the assist motor. The amount of exercise in which a rider engages is entirely dependent upon the extent of the motor assist and the length of the ride.

Nearly all electric bicycles offer user-selectable assist levels. This allows riders to choose a lower level of pedal-assist that requires more exertion by the rider and results in more exercise. Alternatively, when the rider prefers a less strenuous ride, such as when running late to work and not wanting to arrive sweaty, a higher level of pedal-assist can be selected, allowing the rider to travel more quickly with less physical effort.

All electric bicycles can be turned off completely, meaning they provide no electric assist and thus function entirely like conventional pedal bicycles. Some e-bikes can even have both the battery and motor removed to reduce the weight of the bike when operating as a pedal-only bike.

Unlike pedal bicycles though, e-bikes offer the ability to dial in precisely the amount of exercise a rider wishes. This is an enormous advantage over pedal bikes and is often the deciding factor in whether or not a commuter would consider choosing to travel on two wheels instead of four. Obviously, pedal bicycles provide an excellent source of exercise, but most commuters are not seasoned cyclists and are not interested in the high level of exertion required by pedal bikes. The ability for riders to customize the level of electric assist provided by an e-bike is the sole reason that many commuters feel comfortable switching to two wheels. This feeling of a safety net is the confidence boost that riders need to experience cycling as both a form of transportation and also as a leisure activity – something they likely haven't tried since childhood.

Furthermore, the electric assist of an e-bike is often reported as "taking the edge off" of the ride or otherwise keeping the rider at an enjoyable level of exertion instead of pushing the rider to exhaustion. For this reason, many electric bicycle riders discover that they ultimately ride for much longer than they originally anticipated or planned to. Studies have found that the longer period that e-bike riders spend on the bikes in many cases results in similar amounts of exercise compared to pedal bike riders.[5] E-bike riders may not be exerting themselves as strenuously, but are doing so for longer and thus burning similar amounts of calories.

At a time when western societies are struggling with lifestyle-related health epidemics, e-bikes very well may hold the key to our salvation. By 2018, 42.5% of the adult population of the United States suffered from obesity and 73.6% were considered overweight, according to the US Centers for Disease Control and Prevention (CDC) and the National Center for Health Statistics (NCHS).[6]

---

[5] Castro, Alberto, et al. "Physical Activity of Electric Bicycle Users Compared to Conventional Bicycle Users and Non-Cyclists: Insights Based on Health and Transport Data from an Online Survey in Seven European Cities." *Transportation Research Interdisciplinary Perspectives*, vol. 1, June 2019.

[6] Fryar CD, Carroll MD, Afful J. Prevalence of overweight, obesity, and severe obesity among adults aged 20 and over: United States, 1960–1962 through 2017–2018. NCHS Health E-Stats. 2020.

Let that number sink in for a moment. Nearly three of every four adults in the US are overweight.

We often think of this as an American problem and blame an "American lifestyle", but Europe isn't fairing that much better. More than 58% of European adult men and 51% of European adult women are overweight, according to the World Health Organization (WHO)[7].

Consider what that means: significantly over half of all adult Americans and Europeans are overweight. Being overweight is the new normal. Being obese in the United States, which is defined as severely overweight, is nearly the majority condition. By definition, healthy-weight individuals are now *abnormal*.

Such high rates of obesity create enormous burdens, both health-related and financial. According to the CDC, obesity carries increased health risks for type 2 diabetes, coronary heart disease, high blood pressure, high cholesterol, stroke, gallbladder disease, osteoarthritis, breathing problems/sleep apnea, several types of cancers and even several mental illnesses including

---

[7] "Age-Standardized Prevalence of Overweight (Defined as Body Mass Index (BMW) ≥ 25 Kg/m2) in People Aged ≥ 18 Years." *World Health Organization*, World Health Organization, gateway.euro.who.int/en/indicators/h2020_6-overweight/#:~:text=In%20the%20WHO%20European%20Region%20the%20age%2Dstandardized%20prevalence%20of,kg%2Fm2%20for%20obesity).

clinical depression. In fact, the CDC lists obesity as a risk factor for literally "all causes of death".[8]

Beyond the physical cost of obesity, these health consequences carry an immense financial burden as well. The CDC estimated that the health costs associated with obesity in the US were $147 billion in 2008, the last year in which official numbers were available.[9] That year the CDC estimated that obese individuals paid $1,429 more annually for healthcare. Being obese doesn't just cost us our health and years off of our lives, it also costs us real dollars. In countries with universal healthcare, this cost is passed on to all citizens through their taxes. In countries like the US, those fortunate enough to have private health insurance may have many of these costs covered. But for the uninsured, these healthcare costs can be crippling.

While these numbers are frightening, we can again turn to the humble e-bike as a solution. The type of exercise offered by electric bicycles is precisely the type of activity that can help prevent the health impacts suffered by being overweight or obese. According to the WHO, 150 minutes per week of moderately intensive aerobic physical activity results in a 30% reduction in

---

[8] "The Health Effects of Overweight and Obesity." *Centers for Disease Control and Prevention*, Centers for Disease Control and Prevention, 17 Sept. 2020, www.cdc.gov/healthyweight/effects/index.html.

[9] Finkelstein, Eric A et al. "Annual medical spending attributable to obesity: payer-and service-specific estimates." *Health affairs (Project Hope)* vol. 28,5 (2009): w822-31. doi:10.1377/hlthaff.28.5.w822

risk of heart disease, 27% reduction in risk of diabetes and 21-25% reduction in risk of colon and breast cancers.[10] That is the equivalent of a 30-minute e-bike ride per day, 5 days a week. Alternatively, that could also be a 15-minute e-bike ride to work and home each day. Simply swapping a car for an e-bike to get to work could reduce the risk of heart disease by nearly a third.

The use of an electric bicycle as a combination of utilitarian transport and exercise speaks to its effectiveness in both cases. We all know that getting in enough exercise each day can be difficult. Unless sticking to a steady exercise routine, most people don't have a daily reliable source of exercise. But because most people do need to move around their city several times per day, this opportunity perfectly lends itself to incorporating exercise into the daily schedule.

Even if work is too far away to ride an e-bike, or the roads don't support safe cycling (another issue we will discuss shortly), other errands may provide excuses to hop on an electric bike. Quick trips such as visiting the post office or picking up a food order make great excuses to leave the car in the garage and instead ride an e-bike.

The more a rider begins to incorporate an e-bike into his or her life as a transportation tool, the more it begins

---

[10] "Promoting Physical Activity." *www.emro.who.int*, World Health Organization, www.emro.who.int/health-education/physical-activitiy/promoting-physical-activity/All-Pages.html.

to impact the rider's lifestyle. This is the key to achieving sustained health benefits from e-biking. It isn't enough to go on a sporadic electric bicycle ride. Even riding once a week won't provide substantial health benefits. A weekly ride can be a fun break from the world, but it won't significantly impact your health. This isn't about a quick one-time expenditure of calories; the name of the game is lifestyle change. Incorporating a daily e-bike ride as a part of a normal routine is the best way to take advantage of the health benefits of e-biking. Consistent, regular e-bike riding is necessary to impart the cardiovascular fitness that the rest of the body's health is built upon.

The structure of work days for many of us means we spend much of our waking hours desk-bound, rising only to walk down the hall and back. Such sedentary lifestyles are all too common, especially among office workers. With work requiring us to be confined to such small spaces, the act of arriving at work and leaving for home represents one of the few opportunities for movement during an entire day.

Unfortunately, most of us fail to take advantage of this opportunity. Instead, we remain just as sedentary behind the wheel of a car or on the bench of a bus as we were at our desks all day. But an e-bike could provide that much-needed activity, even for short spurts twice a day, that breaks up a monotonous schedule and engages the body in important physical activity.

Incorporating e-bikes as a transportation alternative is a great way to sneak regular exercise into a busy schedule. But for those who have the time for recreation in their schedules, e-bikes offer even more benefits. On top of all the health benefits associated with the type of physical activity that e-bikes can provide, regular e-bike rides are often touted with quality of life and happiness improvements, especially when used for recreation.

Because e-bikes take the edge off of cycling and remove the painful part of the activity, riders are left purely with the enjoyment that cycling offers. Why do young children ride bicycles instead of walking or running? It isn't for transportation. They aren't on a tight schedule and looking to arrive somewhere quickly. No, they ride bikes because they are *fun*. The feeling of gliding along at speed is such a basic joy that cycling is one of the few physical activities enjoyed by nearly every age group. And removing the most arduous level of physical exertion means that the joy of cycling isn't stymied by cramping muscles and gasps for breath.

This impact on the mental health of riders isn't just subjective, it has actually been quantified. A 2018 study published in the psychology journal *The Lancet* found that cycling reduced bad mental health days by 21.6%.[11] In fact, cycling was the second-highest performing

---

[11] Chekroud, Sammi R et al. "Association between physical exercise and mental health in 1·2 million individuals in the USA between 2011 and 2015: a cross-sectional study." *The Lancet. Psychiatry* vol. 5,9 (2018): 739-746. doi:10.1016/S2215-0366(18)30227-X

physical activity in the study, coming in closely behind team sports, which reported a 23.3% reduction in bad mental health days. As important as the physical health benefits of cycling are, the mental health benefits should not be overlooked.

Another large factor impacting mental health is time spent among family. With kids spending more time than ever in front of screens, family time can be hard to come by. But here too, electric bicycles may provide a solution.

Many new e-bike riders become so keen on the sport that they end up convincing their spouses or other family members to join them. It is not uncommon for one e-bike in a garage to be followed by several more as the whole family takes up the new activity together. While some riders surely enjoy the solitude of a pleasant nature ride, the act of engaging in a physical activity as a group can provide added benefits, as evidenced in *The Lancet* study referenced above.

The health benefits of e-bikes are simply so numerous and widespread that it is amazing they aren't more widely marketed as the wonderdrug they are. A veritable panacea, the variable degree of exercise offered by e-bikes is ripe with benefits for the body and the mind.

# Chapter 4: Embracing a massive shift towards e-bikes

The potential for electric bicycles to create a significant betterment of our world is undeniable. From improving the health of our planet to decongesting our cities and even improving ourselves, the technology's benefits span so many levels.

Now that we've recognized the myriad of benefits, it is incumbent upon us to act. The solution is here, but we must embrace it. Adopting e-bikes to the point where we can achieve a massive shift towards mainstream use will require a fundamental change in the way we view transportation.

This shift has already occurred to a lesser degree in many areas of the world. For example, tens of millions of new electric bicycles are sold every year in China. The country has wholeheartedly embraced electric bicycles as a legitimate, standard form of transportation in cities. Of course, e-bikes have not led to the disappearance of the car in China. But they have greatly reduced the number of cars on China's roads by replacing them with smaller, more efficient electric bicycles.

Europe is several years behind China in terms of e-bike adoption, but the continent has already made impressive progress. Western European countries like Germany are leading the way, albeit with a different type of electric bicycle. In China, electric moped-style e-bikes that more closely resemble seated scooters represent the vast majority of models on the road. It is not uncommon to see these e-bikes operating with two, three or even more passengers on the long bench seats. Meanwhile in Europe, single-rider metro-style e-bikes designed for city riding are much more popular.

China's (and to a lesser extent Europe's) embrace of electric bicycles as a routine, common form of alternative transportation has shown that the obstacles to large-scale e-bike adoption are less practical and more cultural. It's not a matter of "Can commuters switch from cars to electric bicycles?" Instead, it is a question of "Will they?" And the answer to that question is firmly rooted in the culture and priorities of a society.

Enter: The United States. For the last few decades, the US has become the land of the SUV. Big cars have ruled supreme and a single driver in a massive vehicle became the epitome of the American dream on wheels. Personal mobility in the form of bicycles and scooters were nothing more than fitness equipment or children's toys. But in 2018 that all changed with the advent of the shared electric scooter. Private companies peppered cities with GPS-tracked electric scooters that could be rented by the minute with a simple phone app.

The concept wasn't entirely new. Bike shares, which offered short-term bicycle rentals in urban areas, had already been in operation for years. But they never caught on in any meaningful way in the US. They solved the problem of bike ownership, providing a cheaper upfront cost and without the concerns of bike maintenance or theft. But they didn't solve the main problem with bikes: most people simply didn't want to pedal them.

However, when the shared electric scooter model was rolled out by large US companies such as Bird and Lime in 2018, something changed. The ease of use of electric power combined with the inherent fun of two-wheeled vehicles saw the electric scooters explode in popularity. The services were still largely used by young riders under 30, but more adults were taking notice and signing up. Suddenly it was no longer strange to see a man in a business suit riding down the street on what looked like a children's toy. Micromobility in the US had just received its first huge shove forward.

By this point, e-bikes had already been growing in popularity in the US, but their sales were measured in the tens of thousands per year – nothing compared to the millions of sales in Europe and the tens of millions in

Asia. As micromobility grew in popularity and shared electric scooters began to help Americans realize they could get around town for pocket change on small electric scooters, e-bike sales began taking off as well.

Then came the biggest shot in the arm to the US e-bike market to date, and largely throughout the world as well: the COVID-19 pandemic. Nearly two years after electric scooters rolled into US cities en masse, lockdowns during the pandemic sent the public scrambling. Suddenly people had time on their hands and were seeking socially distant activities that could get them out of the house and away from crowds. Those who were still required to travel to work sought safer alternatives to crowded public transportation and cheaper alternatives to personal cars. E-bike sales in the US and around the world skyrocketed. Whether for transport, pleasure, utility or any other reason, e-bikes began selling like hotcakes. E-bike companies had empty warehouses across the board. E-bikes were selling out before they even made it onto the shelves.

Demand had changed. Public perception of e-bikes had changed. But cities didn't change. As e-bike sales began to stabilize again after the frenzied rush, cities didn't respond any differently, at least for the most part. Some cities instituted temporary cycling roads or expanded bike lanes into an additional car lane, but the moves were often slowly reversed as lockdowns eased.

The public, especially in the US, had shown the first-ever large embrace of electric bikes and personal transportation, but the cultural shift wasn't met with the support it needed from cities and governments. That support is a critical part of assisting e-bike adoption, especially in these early days of the technology.

Such support can come in a number of different forms. In China, for example, gas-powered scooters and motorcycles are either banned or taxed heavily, which helped support a large-scale modal shift towards electric alternatives. In Europe, governments have provided incentives for citizens to buy electric bicycles. Many countries provide several hundreds of euros. Some provide over a thousand euros to help riders afford electric bicycles. Many European companies provide lease-to-own programs for their employees to ride electric bicycles to work. A few dozen euros per month are charged over a few years, eventually paying off a several thousand euro e-bike at a steep discount.

Some European countries have offered these incentive programs for years and have recently started to ease back or cancel the programs altogether after achieving their goal of boosting the adoption of e-bikes. It was feared that the reduction or termination of such programs would result in a sudden drop in the number of e-bike sales. For the most part that has not been the case. By providing several years of incentives that helped boost the popularity of e-bikes, the public began to accept the growing numbers of e-bikes on the road as any other vehicle. E-bikes became *normal*, which was precisely the point. Even after incentives have been drawn back in some European countries, the popularity of e-bikes has kept sales strong as friends of e-bike riders rush to join the fray and commute on their own new e-bike.

This is exactly what must be done in other countries, such as the US, where e-bike adoption rates are still fairly low. Government incentives are necessary to help boost early adoption rates and get more e-bike riders on the road. As e-bike ridership increases, their riders naturally become evangelizers for the technology. Even passively, without being preachy, e-bike riders demonstrate the advantage of the technology daily when they whizz past cars waiting in long lines of traffic. The more that Americans start to see e-bikes effortlessly gliding by while they themselves are stuck sitting in their car in traffic, the more the idea of e-biking will become interesting to frustrated drivers. It's the chicken and egg problem: people need to see e-bikes being used in order to want to buy them, but more people need to buy them in order for others to see them being used. Governments can lay that egg – they can help in putting more e-bikes on the road, ultimately jumpstarting that cycle.

And of course, governments have much to gain from this as well. When people spend less time stuck in traffic they end up with more time for productivity. When people are exercising and maintaining healthier lifestyles they end up drawing upon fewer government resources to treat health complications brought on by obesity. And when fewer cars use our roads to pollute our air, land and water, the government can spend less money repairing infrastructure or trying to combat impending climate disasters. It is in the government's best interests to act. A few hundred dollars of incentives per person beats a few thousand dollars of medical bills.

As great as it would be to simply buy our way to higher rates of e-bike adoption, the answer is unfortunately not quite that simple. With present infrastructure, cities can only handle so many cyclists. Most cities are designed for cars, with cycling lanes often added as an afterthought. Brave changes are required in many cities to create a more welcoming cycling atmosphere. This includes not just the painting of bicycle lanes on the side of roads, which can create dangerous shared space, but actually protected bike lanes. These lanes can be separated by a number of physical barriers such as parked cars, pylons, planting beds or other objects that can provide utility for the city in addition to physical separations between cyclists and cars.

Even better is to completely ban cars from certain areas of cities. While it sounds drastic, many cities are already doing just that. City centers are becoming car-free zones in favor of walking, cycling and space-efficient forms of personal transportation. While this of course can't work for entire cities, redesigning sections of cities to allow for driving on larger thoroughfares but not in smaller neighborhood centers can provide the best of both worlds. Cars can be used to arrive close to a destination, then riders can park and either walk or ride a personal mobility device such as a folding e-bike that was stored in their trunk for just such occasions.

In fact, the reduction of cars from cities and the creation of protected cycling lanes often go hand in hand. Many cities that were not designed from the outset with personal mobility in mind have found it difficult to update their infrastructure to include safe, dedicated cycling lanes. This is understandable, as most urban roads have no room to expand. Without knocking down buildings to widen roads, there just isn't any more space.

But hopefully the solution here is beginning to become obvious. If space is limited for both cars and bikes, and the ultimate goal is to create more cycling infrastructure, then car space must be reduced. Even if cities can't create car-free zones, reducing the number of lanes dedicated to cars will free up space to create wide, protected cycling paths.

Car traffic may increase in the short term due to the limited car space, but this will eventually hasten the switch to more efficient modes of transportation. The immediate increase in traffic disincentivizes drivers, especially when they see all the electric bicycles and other forms of alternative personal transport flying past them in traffic.

One of the largest obstacles to increased rates of cycling is the perceived danger that cyclists feel. And that perception isn't unwarranted – cycling is unfortunately responsible for more deaths than automobiles on a per-mile basis. Though to say that "cycling is responsible" for such deaths is misleading. In actuality, cars are responsible for the vast majority of those cycling deaths. Cars and cyclists simply don't mix well. While a fender bender between two cars is usually just a nuisance for all parties involved, the same type of accident between a car and a bike can often prove fatal.

If cars and bikes mix so poorly on the same roads, then the need for cycling-specific roads or paths is underscored. And yet it creates another chicken and egg problem. We need to dedicate more space to cyclists, yet there are so many cars on the road that it is difficult to take more space away from them without disrupting cities. Without enough obvious demand for cycling infrastructure, there often isn't sufficient justification for cities to make the switch.

In this case, we again need to create the egg or force the demand for safer cycling infrastructure. A large uptick in cycling, driven largely by the ease of adoption that e-bikes offer, can put more cyclists on the roads and demonstrate a sudden increased demand to city officials. At the same time, more cars are taken off the road as drivers switch to e-bikes. The reduced car load and increased bike load easily make the case for cities to create more cycling infrastructure including dedicated cycling paths and protected bike lanes.

Creating proper cycling infrastructure to encourage increased adoption rates of small-format personal transportation is critical, but such urban planning is an entire field in and of itself that we do not have the space in these pages to explore to the extent that it deserves. But suffice it to say that smart city design can be one of the most effective tools used to encourage cycling as a safer and more effective alternative to cars. The field deserves increased study as an important part of a societal shift of transportation modes.

Lastly, when discussing cycling safety, we need to briefly discuss helmets. There isn't much more to say than "wear one." At the risk of sounding like your mother, the single largest factor affecting the survivability of a cycling accident is whether or not the rider is wearing a helmet. Most cycling fatalities are caused by head injuries. That $20 piece of foam may not look cool but it very well could be the difference between living to 30 or 80.

Ultimately, the rate of e-bike adoption as alternative transportation to private cars is growing at an increasing rate but is still being stymied by the design of our cities. With more emphasis placed on modifying cities to become more cycling-friendly, we can expedite the shift to personal electric transportation and take advantage of the numerous benefits offered by e-bikes and other micromobility vehicles.

# Chapter 5: What can you do about it?

We can talk all day about how cities should be more accommodating to cyclists, but ultimately the responsibility for choosing a more sustainable method of transportation belongs to us. We each make a decision every morning about how we will move around our community, and that decision affects us and everyone around us.

The best way to position yourself to become an e-bike rider as a form of transportation is to design your life to fit a more local perspective. While some people choose to commute dozens of miles in each direction on an electric bicycle, that may not fit the lifestyle of others. Instead, they should consider how some of their trips, perhaps the shorter ones, can be replaced by an electric bicycle.

An e-bike traveling at a modest speed of 15 mph (25 km/h) can complete a 5-mile (8 km) trip in 20 minutes. In many cities, that commute would take just as long or longer by car or bus.

For those of us with longer commutes, consider how an e-bike might be able to supplement a car trip. If you live in the suburbs but work in the city, a folding e-bike in the trunk of your car could make a huge difference in your commute. The highway that takes you into the city surely isn't appropriate for an e-bike commute, but the last few miles through the city could be much improved by an e-bike. It could also allow you to park a few miles out from your destination where parking is cheaper or free, then cycle the rest of the way. In many cities, you'll make better time by skipping the city traffic. You'll also have a fun few minutes to start and end your workday on an e-bike.

Whether or not you use an e-bike as a commuter vehicle to get to work, consider also how you could adopt an e-bike for other travel needs. It will be difficult for many families to entirely rid themselves of a car and replace it with an e-bike for all of their around-the-town errand running. But many more two-car families could instead become one car and one e-bike families. Electric bicycles make excellent second cars for all sorts of utility tasks. Utility-specific e-bikes that have room for cargo boxes or passengers can be a dream for running errands.

Passenger cargo e-bikes are especially useful for ferrying around children. Many families use them to drop kids off at daycare and pick them up at the end of the day. In between, they can be used for grocery shopping or other utility tasks. Long-tail or front-loading electric cargo bikes can often mount soft panniers that expand for carrying cargo and also support passenger seats at the same time, making them the minivans of the electric bicycle world.

Sometimes we will need to consider our own transportation habits and ways that we can change those habits in order to support more e-bike use and less car use. A big step in this direction is to think local. Shop local. Eat local. Drink local. Play local. Work local.

There was a time when neighborhoods and villages contained most or everything their residents needed. While that may no longer be the case in much of the world, if you search for it then you'll likely discover that much of what you really need can be found closer to home than you think. Exploring your own local neighborhood and taking advantage of its resources can help you reduce your travel needs and turn those crosstown trips into shorter e-bike rides to a local corner store or deli.

One of the most common destinations for all of us, and one of the hardest to change for one in closer proximity, is where we work. Our place of work often defines much of our lives, and the ability to work locally is often a luxury that many of us can't afford. But when possible, working close to your home (or alternatively choosing to live closer to your work if agreeable) can be one of the single biggest ways to cut down on your transportation needs and enable you to adopt electric bicycle commuting as a norm.

And while we've largely discussed e-bikes for use in transportation such as commuting or running errands, keep in mind that e-bikes offer so much more than utility. Remember those health benefits we discussed? Those can be achieved regardless of the type of e-bike riding being performed. If you already need to travel to work each day, it simply makes sense to swap your transportation method for one that also offers exercise.

But even if you don't use it for commuting, and instead you adopt e-biking purely for recreational or fitness riding, this still offers numerous benefits. If you don't currently have a daily form of exercise, then I can't recommend enough how much you'll enjoy a daily e-bike ride. It can be hard to fit into a busy schedule, but if you make the time for it, it is 100% worth it. Many people like to start the day with an e-bike ride. The wind in your face is a great way to wake up your senses. The endorphins from light exercise will stay with you for hours as you make your way through your morning at work.

As much fun as it can be, a morning e-bike ride can be a tough sell for those of us who aren't naturally morning people. If you have a hard enough time getting moving in the morning as it is, you might enjoy a daily after-work ride. When I'm stressed, an e-bike ride can be the perfect way to unwind. Pedaling helps me work through that pent-up energy but I don't have to push so hard that I exhaust myself either. There are even days where I'll bookend my work with a ride in the morning and then another in the evening. I'm fortunate enough to live a short ride from the beach, and there's nothing like experiencing the sunrise and then sunset as the backdrop to a beautiful e-bike ride. It's nearly impossible for me to have a bad day when it starts and ends like that.

Each of us doing our part to adopt electric bicycles as alternative transportation is an excellent way to make a measurable positive impact on our world. But it's not the only way. Helping to spread the message is also vitally important. No one wants to be seen as a pushy e-bike proselytizer, but helping to share the benefits of e-bikes with friends can not only accelerate the benefits of higher e-bike adoption rates, it can also help grow your riding group. Riding with friends is a lot of fun, especially on trails and other off-road areas where rides can be leisurely and a group of riders can talk more easily with each other.

Electric bicycles are a bit of a gateway drug. I've met countless people who have told me that after getting an e-bike, many of their family members or friends tried it out and then quickly bought one of their own. The smile I see on the faces of new e-bike riders, especially the first time they hop on the saddle and pedal off, is a true testament to just how much joy an e-bike can offer.

To many people, it's about more than just a better way to travel around a city. E-biking is about finding a healthy and sustainable way to explore our world and experience the child-like fun of riding a bike. That inherent joy makes it easy to spread the e-bike gospel, and it also means no one needs to be pushy to have an effect. Offering a bite of quinoa salad along with a lecture on becoming a vegan is a quick way to clear a room. But offering a ride on an electric bicycle is a quick way to make new friends or bring existing ones closer by starting a new hobby together.

I've been riding e-bikes for over a decade, and for much of that time, I was often the only e-bike rider on the road. As the years have gone by, I see more and more e-bikes around me, to the point where now they are beginning to become commonplace. Even so, I still often share a warm smile or nod of recognition with a stranger as we pass each other on e-bikes. There's a sense of community that comes with these fun alternative transportation machines. They are perfect for sharing, and very few people will ever turn down an offer to take a spin on your e-bike. The test ride may end with a smile and a "thank you". Or it may result in a friend joining the world of e-biking, losing weight, getting healthy, enjoying his or her commute and having fun. And it could all start with that first ride.

# Chapter 6: Finding the right e-bike

No matter the type of riding you plan to do, whether it be transportation, utility, recreation or fitness, choosing the right type of e-bike is critical to getting the most out of the experience. There are several different types of e-bikes on the market that specialize in different niches. Below I'll cover the main categories and where they are best used.

Before getting into the individual categories though, perhaps the largest differentiator in the e-bike market is the type of motor offered, either mid-drive or hub motor. Mid-drive motors place the motor near the pedals and power the rear wheel via the bike's chain or belt. They have the advantage of increased gear range through the motor and can make climbing hills easier. They also have a more comfortable and lower center of mass. Hub motors are placed in the center of the bike wheel, with the spokes directly laced to the motor itself.

Spinning the motor causes the wheel to spin, and the bicycle's pedals and chain are left as a separate system entirely. Hub motors are generally less expensive than mid-drive motors and can be simpler, potentially meaning fewer maintenance concerns and less wear on the bicycle's chain and sprockets.

The second biggest differentiator in e-bikes is whether or not they have a throttle. A throttle is mounted on the handlebars and activated by either twisting the wrist like a motorcycle or pressing a thumb lever. It engages the motor without the rider needing to pedal, effectively operating the e-bike like a moped or low-power motorcycle. They are quite convenient when the e-bike is being used purely as a transportation tool, but offer little in the way of health benefits as they don't require the rider to use the pedals. Most throttle-enabled e-bikes also feature pedal assist modes, meaning the rider can forego the throttle and instead power the e-bike by pedaling while the e-bike's pedal assist sensors help to apply the chosen amount of electric assist.

E-bikes without throttles only offer pedal assist. In many areas of the world, pedal-assist e-bikes are the standard due to regulations outlawing e-bike throttles. In the US, throttle-enabled e-bikes are much more common.

Now with those two main differentiators out of the way, let's examine the different styles of e-bikes available to riders.

## Electric city bikes

Electric city/metro e-bikes, also called electric commuter bikes, are usually designed for urban transport. They generally place an emphasis on efficient riding and thus feature lightweight frames and somewhat narrower tires. E-bikes in general though have a distinct benefit in tire selection, as they can take advantage of the traction as well as the ride comfort improvements of slightly wider tires without suffering the same weight penalties that pedal bikes must contend with. When it comes to city e-bikes, many have basic commuter essentials included, such as lights, fenders and racks. Some are designed to offer a more comfortable and upright seating position, while others provide a more tucked ride that offers better aerodynamic efficiency at higher speeds.

City and commuter e-bikes are a great option for commuters looking to replace car trips with an e-bike trip. The bikes are designed to be rugged enough for everyday use as a dependable daily driver, but also light enough that they can be maneuvered easily, even up stairs or into an elevator.

Commuter e-bikes often lack any form of suspension, meaning no rear suspension or suspension fork. This tradeoff can make for a lighter and more durable bike with fewer moving parts, but at the expense of reduced comfort. To make up for the lack of suspension, riders can add a suspension seat post, a more comfortable saddle or try sticking to smoothly paved bike lanes and roads.

## Folding electric bikes

Folding electric bicycles often blend with this category of commuter e-bikes, but not always. Folding e-bikes are generally a bit heavier due to the added complexities of a built-in folding mechanism. Many lightweight folding e-bikes still exist though, and they make great last-mile vehicles that can be stored in a car's trunk or folded when brought onto a subway or train, extending the rider's range to and from public transit hubs.

Folding e-bikes can also be great for recreation as they allow riders to transport the bike to a popular riding destination in a car's trunk. Ideally, e-bikes would be used to cut down on car use, but sometimes riders don't live close to ideal riding areas and need to transport their e-bike to a trailhead. In this case, folding e-bikes can make it useful to fit the e-bike more easily in a vehicle.

The folding nature of such e-bikes also makes them popular for pilots, RV drivers and boat owners. A folding e-bike can be stored onboard without taking up much space, and can then be used once the owner reaches a destination and wants to travel around away from the larger plane, RV or boat.

One downside to folding electric bicycles is that they sometimes make compromises including smaller wheel sizes and smaller batteries. These design choices make the bikes easier to fold, but they can somewhat reduce the ride comfort or range of the e-bike. Many riders swear by smaller wheels though, so it often comes down to a matter of personal preference.

## Electric mountain bikes

Electric mountain bikes, whether full suspension or front suspension-only, are generally designed more for recreational riding. They have larger, more rugged frames that are designed to handle the abuse of riding off-road and bouncing over obstacles. There are many styles of electric mountain bikes that cover different types of riding, such as downhill, cross country or trail riding, but they all share many of the same basic characteristics. They usually offer a more tucked riding posture, wider handlebars, heavier frames and larger, more aggressive tires.

## Fat tire electric bikes

Electric fat tire bikes often share many similarities with electric mountain bikes, yet include much wider fat tires. "Fat tires" don't have an exact definition, but usually begin with widths of at least 4" wide. They were preceded by tires in the 3" range, which are usually referred to as balloon tires, but have since faded in popularity.

Electric fat tire bikes sometimes offer suspension and are designed for more recreational riding. Their fat tires are specialized for soft or loose terrain like sand, snow and dirt. Even though their primary use is for more recreation-oriented riding, many people have adopted fat tire e-bikes for commuter roles and find that the fat tires help improve the ride on pockmarked urban streets. Hitting a piece of lumber or other large obstacles could be hazardous on small bicycle tires, but fat tires can easily roll over such debris without much of an impact on the rider.

## Electric cruiser bikes

Electric cruiser bikes adopt cruiser frames, which are known for their wide saddles, upright seating position and swept-back handlebars. These are some of the most comfortable electric bicycles as they are designed for easy riding, hence the cruiser name. While they can make fine commuter or fitness e-bikes, they are best used for recreational and leisure riding. A beachfront path or boardwalk is the classic cruiser bike setting, but they are also great for fairly smooth nature trails and other leisurely riding locations.

## Cargo/utility e-bikes

Electric cargo bikes and utility e-bikes are a specialty branch that are perhaps most similar to city e-bikes but deserve their own unique category. The frames are designed to be stronger to accommodate carrying heavier loads, and the components such as brakes, tires and bearings are often upgraded to withstand the increased stress of riding with extra cargo or passengers.

They generally offer a wide range of accessories that can be installed on the bike, such as passenger seats/rails either for adults or children, cargo boxes, soft-sided pannier bags, baskets and racks. They usually have somewhat larger tires, though not necessarily fat tires. They are urban-optimized, meaning fairly smooth tire treads and usually feature included lights and fenders. Electric cargo or utility e-bikes are perfect for riders looking to replace a second car for around-the-town trips and running errands. With the right cargo accessories, they can be used to purchase groceries, make hardware store runs, carry surfboards, ferry around several children or many other everyday utility tasks.

## Electric road bikes

Electric road bikes are designed almost purely for fitness riders. They are the lightest style of e-bike and usually feature lower power motors and smaller batteries. They almost never include a throttle as they are intended to be used as exercise tools. Many electric road bikes provide an assistance level that is barely more powerful than a human rider can provide, with the emphasis being on the battery serving in a purely helping capacity, assisting the rider as they provide most of the propulsion. Many riders find that they use minimal or no electric assistance for much of the ride, and dip into the battery more when climbing hills or for returning home when the rider is exhausted.

Road e-bikes take more getting used to if the rider isn't already accustomed to them, as they require a much more tucked riding position. They also usually feature narrower saddles and drop bars, both of which can feel odd or uncomfortable to riders who are accustomed to more city or leisure-style bicycles.

## Electric mopeds

Electric mopeds are found on the opposite end of the spectrum from electric road bikes. They are often heavy, bulky and designed to be operated mainly by the throttle. Moped-style e-bikes often adopt vintage styling cues and feature long bench seats that can be more comfortable than a typical bicycle saddle but that aren't always optimized for pedaling. Some electric moped-style bikes are better suited to pedaling than others, but all make geometry sacrifices in order to offer the laid-back moped frame.

Most electric mopeds include higher power motors and larger batteries, and nearly all use wider tires if not fat tires. They generally have smaller diameter tires though, with a 20" x 4" tire size becoming quite common in the electric moped market. Large headlights, built-in horns and other motorcycle-like components are common on electric mopeds. More expensive models often feature front or full suspension, but many electric mopeds include no suspension at all, relying instead on fat tires and plush seats to cushion the ride.

If you've never ridden an electric bicycle before, it is highly recommended to visit an e-bike dealer in your area and test out several styles before buying one. There are so many different e-bike styles that most riders are likely to find several that are better suited for their comfort and riding style.

In addition to electric bicycle dealers, many e-bikes are sold online via direct-to-consumer websites. These companies can often offer better prices by cutting out the middleman and cutting costs associated with running a physical retail location. However, they can also make it harder to get help if you ever need service or support. Some of the larger direct-to-consumer electric bicycle companies offer several support options including detailed online guides or even mobile van services that can send an e-bike technician to your door. But the smaller companies may lack these services, so it is important to research what type of customer support options a company offers before purchasing an electric bicycle.

# Chapter 7: Are e-bikes the only answer?

This entire manifesto has focused on only one type of alternative transportation, the simple and unassuming electric bicycle. But if our goal is to replace cars and find more sustainable solutions to move people around their communities, are e-bikes the only option?

Of course not.

There are plenty of interesting alternatives to cars. An entire new field known as the micromobility industry has sprung up to answer this call for more sustainable personal transportation. E-bikes were one of the first, but the sheer number of alternatives is mind-blowing, and seemingly every week we see some new and sometimes strange entry into the market.

As an international journalist that travels the world covering all sorts of personal transportation solutions,

I've seen and tried just about every one of them out there. Many of them have unique advantages and interesting features that could make them more applicable to certain people. But I have found that by and large, electric bicycles provide the best combination of advantages and capabilities for the widest number of users.

And while I would place electric bicycles at the top of the list, they of course carry their own unique disadvantages and thus they may not be right for everyone. Instead, certain riders might find some of these alternatives to be more useful for their own needs.

Electric motorcycles have two main advantages over electric bicycles: they can travel faster and farther. Electric bicycles are limited mostly to the same areas where bicycles can safely ride. But electric motorcycles can travel just about anywhere a car can, and often in even more places. While I've ridden plenty of fast electric bicycles that can reach speeds of 40 mph (64 km/h) or more, electric motorcycles really open the door to personal electric commuting. Highway-capable electric motorcycles can be ridden much faster than any interstate speed limit and thus provide access to any road that a car can travel on.

When I need to travel longer distances and on faster roads, I prefer riding an electric motorcycle. They offer a similar style of fun and excitement to electric bicycles, though cranked up several clicks thanks to their higher power motors and improved handling. Most electric motorcycles made today have highway ranges nearing 100 miles (160 km) or more and city ranges that can be almost twice as much. For city use, electric motorcycles have vastly more range than is necessary, but highway riding can drain the batteries more quickly and make motorcycle touring trickier on electric motorcycles. Fast charging can refill a battery to nearly full in around half an hour, though this still can't compare to the speed of a gas tank fill-up. Most people don't use electric motorcycles for touring or cross-country trips, but instead as a car replacement when commuting to work. Their ability to reach highway speeds and then lane split in cities also means that suburbanites can significantly reduce their commute time compared to a car by taking the highway into the city and then blowing past the traffic.

It is important to note that electric motorcycles, just like all motorcycles, carry significantly more risk to riders. I fully promote motorcycles as responsible and sustainable vehicles that can help reduce traffic and improve our cities, but I don't deny that they come with a safety tradeoff. Riders absolutely *must* be more aware of their surroundings than they would be in a car. Rider training courses are usually required to receive a motorcycle license, and I highly recommend them even if they aren't. Safe riding comes from a combination of education and experience. The former can best be obtained from those with the latter, and so enrolling in a motorcycle training course is highly recommended for new riders that want to switch from four wheels to two.

For those that don't need the high power of an electric motorcycle but still want an electric vehicle that is larger and more capable than an electric bicycle, seated electric scooters can make great alternatives. These Vespa-style scooters, sometimes referred to as mopeds, offer higher speeds, more power and more range than electric bicycles, but are usually well below the performance figures of electric motorcycles.

The lower performance also means they cost a fraction of typical electric motorcycle prices. They still require much of the same knowledge to operate safely though, so new scooter and moped riders will also benefit from a motorcycle training course.

One of the main advantages of electric scooters compared to electric motorcycles, besides the lower price, is the added utility. I ride an electric scooter often and find that it is one of the best ways to carry larger items around town. While it can't compare to the cargo capacity of a car, scooters offer both trunk space and space between your feet. This can be incredibly useful when shopping, as multiple bags can be hung from a bag clip or placed at the rider's feet. Motorcycles can also be mounted with storage boxes, but many riders refrain from adding them due to their bulky shapes making it harder to mount the bike and detracting from the overall appearance. But utility-focused scooter riders often care less about image and more about how much cargo they can carry. Also, scooters usually have room for a second rider, which is quite convenient when traveling with a partner or friend.

Both electric scooters and electric motorcycles offer sustainable, fun transportation solutions that provide enough speed and power to replace most car trips. But the higher costs compared to electric bicycles put them out of the budgets of many riders. Also, their higher power motors and longer-range batteries often aren't necessary for purely urban riders.

Instead, smaller electric kick scooters that are ridden standing up can sometimes be a better urban transportation solution than a full-size seated electric scooter or electric motorcycle. Standing electric scooters don't offer the same cargo or utility advantages as seated electric scooters or even electric bicycles, but they are much smaller, lighter and cheaper. These advantages alone can make them more suitable for many urban commuters that prioritize a lightweight vehicle for short trips that can be lifted and carried by hand.

Standing electric scooters come in a vast array of types, with many options for features like suspension, lighting, and all-wheel-drive modes. These electric scooters usually prioritize lightweight designs and folding stems to make the scooters easy to pick up and move around. For riders that only need a simple form of urban transportation for shorter trips and that don't need to carry more than what fits in a backpack, electric scooters can be one of the most cost-effective options available.

Other less common alternatives in the lightweight micromobility category include electric skateboards, self-balancing scooters with a single wheel and even self-propelled vehicles like pedal bicycles and kick scooters. Each come with their own advantages and disadvantages. While electric skateboards are the smallest and lightest options, they are also more dangerous due to the low stability and tiny wheels. And just like electric scooters or motorcycles, they offer almost zero fitness benefits.

Self-propelled alternatives like pedal bicycles and kick scooters are excellent for added exercise, but can be exhausting to riders who aren't in sufficient shape to operate them for an entire commute or perhaps just can't manage them over a large hill in the middle of a commute. Even for those in good shape, the exertion can mean the rider arrives at his or her destination sweating heavily, which may not be acceptable. And of course one of the healthiest and cheapest solutions is simply walking. Choosing to walk to a destination should never be discounted, though factors like weather and distance often make walking impractical.

So while there are many different options for alternative transportation in the micromobility industry, I believe that electric bicycles provide the best combination of advantages and include the fewest disadvantages. I've personally owned, ridden and tested all of the different types of personal transportation options I've described in this chapter, and each can be fun and effective. But none offer the combination of affordability, stability, utility and enjoyment that I've experienced with electric bicycles. Each has a place in the larger micromobility ecosystem, but e-bikes are simply the broadest option for the widest number of people and are likely the best option if a rider can choose only one form of alternative transportation.

Any personal mobility device that helps displace cars from the road and reduces a person's total carbon footprint from transportation is a huge step in the right direction. E-bikes likely hold the key to maximizing that impact, but they are far from the only option available to city dwellers.

# Chapter 8: Common arguments against e-bikes

As an advocate for electric bicycles that has worked in the industry for well over a decade, I've run into many common criticisms of e-bikes. Some of these arguments have their merits, while others are based on misconceptions or misinformation. It is important to address the technology's criticisms head-on, both the legitimate and the illegitimate.

One common argument against e-bikes is that they are for the lazy. The idea goes that if someone really wants to enjoy the benefits of cycling, he or she would ride a pedal bike.

While I don't disagree that pedal bicycles are themselves an incredible form of alternative transportation, the main issue is that they simply have too high of a barrier to entry compared to electric bicycles. Very few car drivers are interested in switching to a pedal bicycle and undergoing the long process of building up enough fitness to take the pain out of commuting on a pedal bicycle. Those who are bitten by the fitness bug and pull their old bicycle out of the garage to begin an exercise regimen are often discouraged when they are reminded just how hard it is to hop on a bicycle and travel long distances without first developing sufficient cardiovascular fitness.

Even for those that are fit enough to use a pedal bike as their main form of transportation, pedal bikes still don't offer many of the advantages of electric bicycles. They aren't capable of maintaining the same speeds over long distances, they can't carry the same loads (think cargo e-bikes or passenger-carrying utility e-bikes), and the ones designed to be sufficiently light and efficient to truly reduce the cycling effort required often cost even more than a decent electric bicycle.

I personally run 30 to 45 minutes per day, and I don't think anyone would consider me "lazy." But when I ride a pedal bike I feel sluggish and the experience just isn't as much fun. Riding an e-bike for me isn't a solution to laziness, it is simply a more enjoyable way to cycle, even when I am already in good physical shape.

Fitness riders on pedal bikes will also claim that e-bikes are for the lazy because e-bikes supposedly don't provide a sufficient workout when a motor is assisting the rider. This notion is simply incorrect and has been proven so in countless studies. Pedal-assist electric bicycles that require the rider to pedal in order to activate the motor don't offer the same intensity of exercise as a pedal bike, but still significantly improve cardiovascular fitness. The ride isn't as strenuous, but it still provides plenty of exertion on the rider's part. Some studies have even found that because e-bike riders don't tire as quickly, they actually burn *more* calories on rides by staying out longer and causing the body to work with an elevated heart rate for longer periods of time. If a rider has the fitness to perform long rides on a pedal bicycle, that is great. They are sure to have a great workout. But most people don't possess that fitness level, and instead, find that an e-bike allows them to get a satisfactory workout that would otherwise not be possible for them on a pedal bike.

While pedal bicycles are also great forms of alternative transportation and are incredibly useful as fitness tools, the number of people willing to adopt them pales in comparison to those ready to commit to an e-bike. Electric bikes simply lower the barriers to entry from multiple directions at once, opening more doors for people to enjoy the benefits of cycling.

Unfortunately, one of the main groups of e-bike detractors are actually pedal cyclists, specifically old-school cyclists. An unfortunate number among this group have long considered e-bikes as a form of "cheating." This is part of a larger problem of gatekeeping: They see cycling as a walled community into which riders must earn their stripes through the arduous act of pedal cycling.

The problem here is hopefully obvious: that cycling isn't meant to be an exclusive sport – it should be an inclusive activity. There are so many different types of cycling: recreational, fitness, transportation, utility, etc. If an e-bike rider tried to enter the Tour de France then I might agree that could be problematic. But short of that, pedal cyclists who advocate against increased e-bike adoption are simply trying to preserve their own personal vision of what cycling is to them, instead of realizing what cycling could be for the world.

Another argument against electric bicycles is that they aren't actually a zero-emission alternative to cars since they need to be charged with electricity, which itself has a large carbon footprint. The argument goes that riding an e-bike simply replaces a car's tailpipe emissions with a power plant's smokestack emissions.

This is largely based on a misconception of the efficiency of electricity generation. While it is true that electricity generated from coal-fired power plants and other fossil fuel-based sources creates its own carbon emissions, countless studies have debunked the myth that electric vehicles are just as "dirty" because of these power plant emissions. First of all, even if an electric car uses entirely coal-fired power plants as an electricity source, the emissions are significantly lower than internal combustion engine cars on a per-mile basis. And electric bicycles are around 10x more efficient than electric cars, meaning even when entirely using so-called "dirty" electricity, the carbon emissions are significantly lower than any internal combustion engine-based transportation.

But the reality is that e-bikes rarely use entirely fossil fuel-generated electricity, as renewable energy in the form of solar, wind and other zero-emission alternatives is an increasingly large component of global electricity generation. This means that electric bicycles are only becoming more efficient each year and contributing even less to carbon emissions as time progresses.

Yet another environmental-based argument against electric bicycles questions how sustainable the products are themselves. While using an electric bicycle can produce little to zero emissions depending on where the electricity is generated, producing the electric bicycle is not nearly as clean. Manufacturing the many components, including the frames, motors, batteries, tires, brakes, paint, and other parts still contribute to global emissions.

In this case, it is important to consider both the type of electric bicycle and the emissions it offsets. A life cycle analysis tells us the total impact of an electric bicycle from its production all the way through its use and eventually its disposal. A higher-quality electric bicycle may last many times longer than a cheap electric bicycle, and thus its carbon emissions from production can be offset by its longer useful life.

Alternatively, a cheap electric bicycle that may only last a year before falling apart can be problematic in that it would require a new e-bike to be produced every year. These cheaper electric bicycles can be attractive to new riders because they fit more constrained budgets, but it is important to consider how a higher quality electric bicycle might pay for itself over time, both in terms of the financial cost of buying multiple cheaper e-bikes as well as the emissions cost of producing several e-bikes.

The emissions offset by an electric bicycle should also be considered. While an e-bike purchased purely for recreation or fitness likely won't offset any car-based emissions, an e-bike purchased for transportation could have a significant reduction in a rider's total carbon footprint. If an electric bicycle can replace a car, then the vastly larger emissions associated with the production and use of that car can also be replaced. This offsetting results in a net reduction of carbon emissions, even if the e-bike itself comes with a carbon price tag associated with its production.

Lastly, one very important criticism of electric bicycles is related to safety. Detractors argue that electric bicycles simply aren't safe. This argument comes in a number of forms, such as quoting the higher fatality rate of cyclists compared to car drivers or citing the risks to pedestrians and other cyclists.

These are legitimate concerns that shouldn't be ignored. Some issues related to the safety of electric bicycles lie in the hands of e-bike riders themselves, while others are outside of our personal control.

When considering the higher injury and fatality rate of cyclists compared to cars, one has to consider *why* these cyclists are being injured and killed. While single-rider accidents occur more frequently than we would like, especially in recreational riding such as mountain biking, they are rarely fatal. Instead, fatal bicycle accidents are usually the result of collisions with cars. As we previously discussed, one of the biggest factors impacting the safety of electric bicycles is the development of safer infrastructure that separates cyclists and cars. Until safer infrastructure exists, riders of e-bikes and pedal bikes alike assume the higher risk inherent in mixed modal roads.

Some steps can be taken by the e-bike rider personally, such as wearing high-visibility clothing, a proper fitting helmet and adopting riding styles that emphasize defensive riding. But the creation of protected cycling infrastructure is the most significant step that cities can take to reduce cycling injuries and deaths.

It isn't only the safety of e-bike riders that concerns some detractors, however. There is also an argument that e-bikes are dangerous to others because they travel at higher speeds and can catch pedestrians and other slower-moving cyclists off guard. The biggest issue is on mixed-use trails, where higher-speed electric bicycles can often come flying around blind corners, potentially colliding with hikers and other cyclists. For this reason, many trails ban electric bicycles or sometimes ban throttle-enabled e-bikes that more easily reach higher speeds.

This argument has some merit, and it is largely incumbent upon e-bike riders themselves to ride safely, especially when on mixed-use and/or crowded trails. No one wants to go out for a pleasant morning hike only to be hit head-on by 250 pounds of meat and metal. But e-bikes also aren't the problem here; the true problem is riders. Irresponsible riders can ruin trail access for all by endangering innocent lives. We don't blame cars for car accidents, we blame their drivers. Blaming e-bikes is easy. Educating riders is harder, but it is the correct solution to this problem. And if necessary, enforcement of riding laws and regulations will need to be stepped up to reign in irresponsible riders.

Perhaps one of the most valid arguments against large-scale adoption of electric bicycles is the open-ended question of their utility in sub-optimal weather conditions. There are few things more fun than a beautiful, sunny afternoon cruising on an electric bicycle. But the smiles quickly fade when riders are running late to work on a cold and rainy morning while pedaling against a headwind full of stabbing rain droplets.

The three main weather impediments to electric bicycle use are usually rain, low temperatures and snow/ice conditions.

When people hear that I commute almost exclusively by electric two-wheelers, I often get the question "what happens when it rains?" They are rarely satisfied when I answer "I get wet."

Personally, I'm a bit of a pragmatist. I also adapt to whatever situation I'm in. If it's wet out, I'm wet. I'll eventually dry off, and luckily our species has evolved with a waterproof lining. But of course most people aren't as ready to simply go with the flow as I am. Fortunately for the majority of society, we have the technology to make commuting by e-bike in the rain both dry and tolerable.

Waterproof riding suits exist and they work extremely well. There are many different options available, but the two main styles are separate rain jackets and pants, or a combined rain suit. Good quality versions of both can keep you bone dry while still offering breathability. I tend to prefer a complete rain suit that I can slip in and out of like a onesie. I can throw it on over my clothes and only have one piece of gear to deal with later. The downside is that rainsuits can look a bit funny, like an astronaut on a bike or worker wearing a bunny suit in a computer chip factory. Some people also prefer the ability to pick and choose separate rain jackets and pants that offer more versatility and can be more fashionable than a one-piece rain suit.

Footwear in the rain can be tricky. Fully-waterproof shoes are available, and some riders just stick to rainboots. Sometimes I'll simply wear securely strapped sandals - choosing to not engage in the staying dry battle at all. The sandals dry quicker than shoes and I can swap them for dry shoes and socks from my bag when I arrive at my destination.

When it comes to carrying cargo or personal effects, many decent backpacks come with a rain cover, and the same goes for bicycle specific pannier bags. There are also generic rain covers that fit a variety of bags. Rain isn't a new problem, and bag makers found solutions years ago. Most rain covers are brightly covered, offering extra safety when the rain limits visibility.

There are also rain covers for helmets, but I tend to forgo them. E-bike riders can already wear helmets with fewer vents as they don't need as much cooling air. In fact I usually wear a skateboard helmet with minimal vent holes. For long-haired riders, a helmet cover can keep your helmet largely waterproof and prevent the annoyance of waiting several hours for long hair to dry.

Perhaps the best option to stay dry while e-biking in the rain is to use an enclosed e-bike. There are several electric velomobiles or bicycle-car e-bikes that have partially or fully enclosed cabins. They are more expensive, but offer a dry way to commute in the rain. They also have other advantages such as more cargo space, a more comfortable seated riding position and higher stability thanks to their three or four-wheeled construction.

But rain isn't the only weather-related barrier to e-bike commuting. Many people fear they'll need to pack away their e-bike in the winter when the temperature drops. While this will largely depend on each rider's preferences and ability to withstand the cold, proper preparation makes cold-weather e-bike commuting nearly as easy as fair-weather riding.

Much of the same gear you'd use to bundle up on a cold day will keep you warm on an e-bike. A good jacket and pants are crucial, but gloves and footwear can't be overlooked. The wind-chill effect of riding quickly will have an even further chilling effect on e-bike riders, especially on the extremities such as the hands and feet. The act of pedaling can help keep riders warmer than they'd expect, though the body normally stores this heat closer to the core while the extremities are left to fend for themselves when it gets exceedingly cold. That's another good reason to invest in a good pair of gloves.

In general, the layering method is a good one for cold weather riding, especially so that an outer layer can be peeled off after the rider begins to warm up from a few minutes of pedaling.

One last bit of advice for cold weather e-bike riding is to use a neck gaiter or tube scarf. You don't need a fashionable wool noose that dangles around while riding and then takes up too much space in a bag. You can instead use a simple neck gaiter that you can slide over your head to keep your neck warm. I tuck mine into my jacket collar and pull the top over my face up to my nose. Clipping my helmet strap over the fabric secures it on my face. I can often get my ears into it too, though an ear warmer band or ear muffs can accomplish the same thing if the tube scarf doesn't cover them. With this method, I'm left with just a strip of skin exposed around my eyes, meaning almost my entire body is out of the cold wind. A balaclava will also work, though isn't as multi-use as a neck gaiter.

In addition to preparing the body for cold weather, the bike must also be prepared if being ridden in areas where ground temperatures fall below freezing. Winter and summer tires are quite different, and using the wrong ones can be dangerous. Winter tires will grip the road better in icy or slushy conditions. In seriously icy conditions, studded tires can be used. Many have removable studs that can be screwed on for mornings when ice is present, then removed for nicer days without requiring a complete tire change.

Icy roads also usually mean salty roads. Salt is a great way to degrade your e-bike, either through rusting out components or short-circuiting electrical contacts. Avoid riding through puddles of melted snow or ice on the road, as they can often be full of salt water. It is impossible to completely avoid all salt spray, but reducing it will make it easier to clean your bike afterwards.

When riding in salty conditions, you should clean your e-bike after each ride. Use fresh water to wash off salt, then dry the bike if possible. Avoid pressurized water that can force its way into components. If running water isn't available, a wet cloth is better than not washing the e-bike at all.

These extra steps that are necessary for riding in sub-optimal weather conditions may sound like a lot of extra work, but consider that you'd already be doing most of them even without an e-bike. If you were driving a car in any city where roads regularly freeze, you'd generally be expected to use winter tires when temperatures drop below freezing. You'd already be wearing cold weather gear in lower temperatures, even as a pedestrian, and you'd likely wear rain gear when the skies open up. Riding in such conditions may require slightly better gear, but it is only a marginal step further than most people will already be taking.

And ultimately if riders choose to leave their e-bike in the garage when the weather isn't great, that's not the worst thing either. Every car trip that an e-bike replaces is a step in the right direction, so if a driver can replace most or all car trips during the three nicer seasons of the year, it will still go a long way to helping reduce the negative impacts of fossil fuel-based transportation.

Like any technology that promotes change, e-bikes can be a divisive subject surrounded by numerous arguments. There is no end to the creativity I've seen used to craft arguments against electric bicycles. But while there do exist some legitimate concerns surrounding e-bikes, many of the arguments come from either the ill-informed or the ill-willed.

Legitimate arguments, such as those related to safety, often have solutions that are already well known. The hard part is the implementation. That is up to us.

# Chapter 9: Where do we go from here?

My goal in writing this manifesto has been to bestow upon you the thoughts and opinions that I have crafted over many years of riding and advocating for electric bicycles.

The world we live in faces no shortage of crises. In fact, on particularly rough days I find myself wavering back and forth regarding whether humanity even possesses the ability to reverse the damage we've done. We've simply become so efficient at destroying the planet we live on, and through that process, damaging ourselves as well.

But even in the darkest of times when I wonder if we're already staring down the barrel of a foregone conclusion, I'm still amazed at how one of my deepest passions, a simple and humble electric bicycle, neatly molds itself into a solution to so many of our most dire problems.

The transportation industry is one of the largest contributors to global climate change. And yet I stand here, looking at this fun and simple little e-bike, amazed to see how it has the ability to help millions of people transition away from large polluting vehicles. It offers up much of the same utility as conventional methods of transporting us from point A to B, then loads several cherries on top in the form of helping riders save time, money and potentially years of their lives.

The worldwide medical industry is so focused on the treatment of ailments and disease that the idea of working to head off and actually *prevent* conditions like heart disease, obesity and diabetes gets comparatively trivial resources. Yet this fun and simple little e-bike before us can hold the key to helping billions of people adopt healthier lifestyles, potentially fending off horrible diseases and literally adding years (good, enjoyable years!) to people's lives.

Over the last decade I've watched as e-bike adoption rates have climbed, and I've attempted to play my own role in helping grow those numbers even higher. It's a task that I've dedicated countless hours to and has become something of my life's work up to this point. But I can only do so much by myself.

This isn't about me, it is about *we*. It is up to us.

You and I together are the key to solving so many of these issues. And your family. And your friends. And their friends.

E-bikes hold the answer. Their impacts can benefit people all around the world. The same e-bike that can help you get back into fitness can also help a cash-strapped entrepreneur open a door-to-door business or help a single mom turn a three-train commute to work into a 30-minute e-bike ride, ultimately spending more time each day with her family. E-bikes can bring transportation equity to low-income neighborhoods, can bring healthy lifestyles to riders everywhere and can simply serve as a way to brighten a day with a leisurely and relaxing ride.

So many advantages of e-bikes can be enjoyed by everyone, not just the riders themselves. Cleaner air, reduced carbon emissions helping to slow down the effects of climate change, reduced urban grime, less traffic – all of these are advantages that impact you each time your neighbor rides an e-bike. Now imagine if you could create those effects plus enjoy all of the personal benefits that come with e-biking as well.

All that it takes is to try. Try an e-bike. Go for a test ride. Visit an e-bike shop. Borrow one from a friend. Experience the ride for your first time and you'll instantly understand the power of such a simple little machine.

If you've already discovered the benefits and joys of e-biking, considering sharing it with others. Let friends and family try your e-bike. Or if you're able to, consider gifting the independence of an e-bike to someone in need. A local student that can't afford a car but needs a way to get to school, a family with only one car that struggles to meet their transportation needs, or a friend or loved one that wants to become healthier but can't find a form of exercise that they can stick with – there are so many people who could benefit from the gift of an e-bike.

The largest barrier that exists to the continued adoption of electric bicycles and their use as alternative forms of transportation isn't cost or supply or awareness; it's getting butts on seats. I swear to you, go watch someone take their first ever ride on an electric bicycle and you're almost guaranteed to see a child-like grin on their face. It's like a switch has been flipped in their mind. If you've never tried an electric bicycle yourself, then I all but promise you'll experience this yourself too – an involuntary smile and child-like joy from your very first ride.

If you haven't been bitten by the e-bike bug yet, then it isn't too late. When is the best time to plant a tree? Twenty years ago. When is the second-best time? Today.

# Acknowledgments

If you had told me twelve years ago that I would one day work in the electric bicycle industry, specifically in helping create meaningful change in our world through the use of e-bikes, I wouldn't have believed you.

I also would have asked you, "what's an electric bike?"

A few weeks later I would end up meeting Thorin Tobiassen and Max Pless, two college friends of mine who helped teach me about the technology of e-bikes as well as cycling in general, and who helped me discover the broader cycling world. Together we dove headfirst down the e-bike rabbit hole, digging it deeper at times when we didn't find it to our liking. I am eternally grateful for the countless hours we spent building, tinkering and breaking our way through those early days in the wild west of electric bicycles. Not all of our projects succeeded, but they made us who we are today.

I would like to acknowledge my parents, who raised me to always seek answers to my questions and then to use my knowledge for the betterment of the world. They provided me with the values, resources and education I needed to enter the world on the right foot and headed in the right direction.

Last but most certainly not least, my wife Sapir also deserves a huge debt of gratitude. If it wasn't for her supporting the two of us (or three of us if you count the dog) for years while I was playing with bikes like a child, I never would have developed the career I have today. She believed in me when others didn't and she enabled me to follow my dreams.

# Author Bio

Micah Toll is an award-winning writer, engineer and entrepreneur specializing in light electric vehicles and lithium-ion batteries. He is the author of Amazon #1 best-selling books *DIY Lithium Batteries*, *DIY Solar Power* and *The Ultimate DIY E-Bike Guide*.

He is based out of Tel Aviv, Israel, where he lives with his wife and dog, but travels the world speaking, writing and covering light electric vehicles. His electric bike videos and articles receive millions of views per month online.

When he isn't riding or writing about electric bikes, he can be found slacklining, running, hiking or sinking into the couch watching a mediocre TV show.

Made in the USA
Monee, IL
29 May 2023